Contents

Projects

Words

Difficult words are explained on p. 26.

Check

Before you start any project, check to see if there is a safety note (marked !) in the text. This means you need an adult to help you.

Water football

Gareth is going for goal. Will Christopher manage a save? Ask a friend to help you set up a water football pitch like this on a table or a flat surface outside.

You need a ping-pong ball and plastic squeezy bottles. Can you see how Gareth made his goal posts? What could you use outside for lines, instead of tape?

How much water is each team allowed? Make up some rules and test your water football skills.

❗ **This is a wet game – cover up with a plastic apron.**

◀**Moving water turns the huge wheel of this mill. The wheel drives a machine that rubs two flat stones together to grind corn.**

Rollalong bricks

Jamie is trying to move these heavy bricks. Which one do you think is going to move first?

He has tied yellow elastic bands, both the same length, to the blue strings. The stretch of the elastic measures the **force**. Which arm is pulling with more force?

You could measure the force you need to move something heavy like this. Do felt-tip rollers make a difference?

! **Mind your toes when carrying heavy things.**

▶**The lifeboat slides on its keel over rollers in the middle of the slipway into the sea.**

7

Trolleys on trial

Nana and Rachel are making trolleys strong enough to carry a brick. Can you see what they are using?

Look at some toy cars and trucks. How are the wheels attached so that they can turn easily and carry a weight?

When Rachel finishes her trolley, will it move as easily as Nana's? Design and make some trolleys to carry a heavy load, and find out.

! Get an adult to make holes in the bottom of your drink cans.

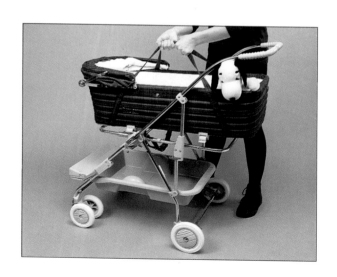

◄Carry-cot transporters need to be strong but light enough to carry folded up. Can you see the axles for the wheels?

9

Slippy sliders

Which toy is sliding down the slope fastest? Ella's car won the first heat. What has won the second heat?

Why not try this game with your toys? You need a board or a table you can lift up slowly at one end. Can you line them up afterwards, as Ella did, fastest first?

Look at the bottom of your toys where they touched the slope. What makes some toys go fast, and others stick?

! **Don't test anything delicate or breakable.**

▶**Marbles are excellent sliders. Ella is using some as** ball bearings **to help these tins spin round.**

Feel the friction

What stops things moving? When two things rub together, we call the force that makes them stick **friction**.

Bronwyn is testing these surfaces by pushing erasers across them. Which things do you think the erasers will slide on? Which will make them stick?

Get some surfaces, and liquids and powders in dishes, and find out about friction for yourself.

! **Use one eraser for each liquid or powder.**

◀**How will oil help Bronwyn's bike to go better? What do you think the** brake pads **might be made of?**

Helter skelter marble run

What will happen when Jamie lets his marble go? He has given it **energy**, lifting it up to the top of the ladder.

Can you see all the things Hannah and Jamie used to make a helter skelter? They had to try lots of different arrangements to get the marbles to land in the pot.

What can you find to make a marble run? What makes your marbles run faster or slower or stops them?

! **Loose marbles on the floor are dangerous.**

▶ **A bob-sleigh run is designed with different slopes and directions to make it exciting – like your marble run.**

15

Magnets move it

Bring two magnets close together. Can you feel the force? Nana and Rachel are using this force to move the models in their shoe-box theatre.

Rachel has glued a small **magnet** to the bottom of each clay model. Nana has stuck a magnet on a stick. What will happen when she moves it around under her stage?

Make your own models to move with magnets.

! **Ask an adult to stick on the magnets with strong glue.**

◀The crane is using a big, round magnet to move scrap iron. What stops the iron from falling off?

Balloon blast off

Blow up a balloon and let it go. As the air rushes back out of the neck, what happens to the balloon?

This balloon is **jet propelled**. Dean makes it zoom along the string by blowing it up and letting go. Can you see how the straw and sticky tape keep it on the string?

Measure how far your balloon rockets go. Which shape of balloon flies furthest?

► **Hot gases come out of the bottom of the firework rockets and push them high into the sky.**

Shadows on the move

Nana's puppet bird flaps its wings when she moves the pink card lever up and down. The other puppets move too.

Can you see the paper fasteners on the back of the rabbit? They are **pivots**: one holds the ear to the rabbit and the other holds the end of the ear to the card strip.

Rachel is fastening an arm on to her witch. What shadow puppet could you design to move with a **lever**?

◀Nana and Rachel's shadow puppets in action. The eyes and mouths are made with coloured tissue paper.

Paper plate gears

Dean cut notches in some stiff paper plates to make **gear** wheels. Can you see how he fastened them through the centre to the cardboard box, so they would fit together?

What happens if he turns that big wheel with his finger? Do all the wheels turn the same way? Could a little wheel turn the big one? Which wheel turns fastest?

Use paper plates to find out about gears yourself.

▶Inside this watch are tiny gear wheels which change the size of forces and movements, and their directions.

Rocket launch

Stretch an elastic band and let one end go. Can you feel the **force** on your fingers? Ella and Daniel are using this force to launch cardboard tube rockets.

Daniel is taping a paper clip to a tin to hold his band in place. As Ella pushes the tube down, her band will stretch. What will happen when she lets go?

Will a short rocket fly further than a long one? Try adding nose cones to your rockets. What happens?

! **Make sure the tin cans have no sharp edges.**

◄**Can you launch a paper glider using an elastic band, sticky tape and a paper clip?**

Words to remember

Axle   The rod which passes through the centre of a wheel.

Ball bearings   Small metal balls fitted inside a device for cutting down friction, often used in axles.

Brake pads   Blocks of rubber which are pressed on to the rim of a wheel to slow it down. This happens when you use the brakes on, for instance, a car or a bicycle.

Energy   Something that machines and animals must have to do work: a car gets its energy from petrol; we get our energy from food.

Force   A push or a pull by one thing acting on another.

Friction   Rubbing. The force that makes things stick as they move over each other.

Gears   A set of wheels with teeth round the edge which mesh together. When the first wheel turns, the second moves with it. Gears often connect a motor to other parts of a machine.

Jet propelled   Driven by a powerful stream of gas which is pushed out behind. Space rockets and jet planes are jet propelled.

Lever   A bar which is fixed at one point along its length (the pivot). It helps us by making a force or a movement bigger.   ·

Magnet   A piece of metal or rock which attracts iron and points north/south when hanging freely.

Pivot   A point on which something turns.

Books for you

Force and Movement by Barbara Taylor (Franklin Watts)
Moving by Brenda Walpole (Kingfisher)
Sliding and Rolling by Terry Jennings (Oxford)

Books to look at with an adult

Moving On Land by Doug Kincaid and Peter S. Coles (Hulton)
Wings, Wheels and Water by K. Little and A. Thomas (Usborne)
Forces in Action by Kathryn Whyman (Franklin Watts)

Places to go

The Science Museum, Cromwell Road, London SW1
The Dome of Discovery, South Rotunda, Govan Road, Glasgow
The Exploratory, Bristol Old Station, Temple Meads, Bristol BS1 6QU
Techniquest, 72 Bute Street, Pier Head, Cardiff CF1 6AA.
All the above have discovery centres with lots of activities.
Centre for Alternative Technology, Machynlleth, Powys SW20 9AZ. Learn about 'green' energy from renewable sources.
Quarry Bank Mill, Styal, Cheshire SK9 4LA. A factory museum, with a powerful wheel in action. Gears to see too.
Rheidol Hydroelectric Scheme, Cwm Rheidol, Aberystwyth, Dyfed SY23 3NB. A water-driven power station open to visitors.

Sparky ideas

Here are some background facts for adults along with some talking points and more ideas for you to try together.

pp 4–5 Water football
- Talk about hydroelectric schemes which turn the energy of falling water into electricity for the National Grid.
- Water moving as waves and tides is another viable, environment-friendly energy source for the future.
- Try the football game with a golf ball. Ask which ball needs the most force to get it moving, and to stop.

pp 6–7 Rollalong bricks
- A load on runners is easier to move because the runners reduce the friction between it and the ground by making the contact area smaller. Look at sledges and ice skates.
- You can find rollers in conveying systems in airports, factories and shops.
- Try taping two felt tips to the base of a brick with parcel tape and measure the force needed to move it.

pp 8–9 Trolleys on trial
- Let the children experiment with other ideas (eg cardboard wheels attached with paper fasteners).
- Other things could make good wheels – old tennis balls, lids of jars, practice golf balls.

pp 10–11 Slippy sliders
- Friction, where the toys touch the slope, is the force which stops them sliding down freely. The winning toys will have smooth bottoms (like the iron) or a small area of contact (like the tin with a metal rim 'runner' on the bottom); or will roll (like the car or a ball).

28

- Ball bearings can be found in the wheel hubs and steering column of a bike. (You can also buy them loose.)

pp 12–13 Feel the friction
- Explain that friction wastes the energy a machine needs for moving and turns it into heat (rub your hands together to check this). Smoothing the surfaces that rub together reduces the friction; so does using a lubricant, like oil or talc.
- A layer of air is another good lubricant. This is how a hovercraft works.
- Friction can also be a useful force. It holds the food on your fork, nails in wood and the threads in your clothes.

pp 14–15 Helter skelter marble run
- Remind the children of what they have already learned about friction and ramps.
- Explain that the force which makes the marble run downwards is the pull between the marble and the Earth (gravity). Lifting the ball up to the top of the run gives it stored energy which it uses to roll down again.

pp 16–17 Magnets move it
- Explain that magnets can push as well as pull. Help the children to find the sides of the round magnets which attract and glue them that way to the stick and puppets.
- The magnets will only be strong enough to move small clay puppets. Papier mâché figures are ideal.
- Try a magnetic fishing game with a friend. Cut out paper fish, slip a paper clip on each one and then see who can fish fastest with a magnet tied to a piece of string.

pp 18–19 Balloon blast off
- Explain that the force of the air rushing out of the neck of the balloon is balanced by an equal force which pushes the balloon in the opposite direction.

- Jet planes and space rockets move forward by pushing out large masses of hot gas behind them at great speed.
- Long, thin balloons should fly further because the streamlined shape reduces the friction with the air.
- Attach card 'fins' to each side of the balloon (like the fins on a space rocket) and see if the balloon goes further.

pp 20–21 Shadows on the move
- Explain that these levers change the way a force acts, turning a small, up-and-down movement of the card strip into a bigger, waving one on the puppet.
- Old railway signals and long-handled garden pruners are worked by levers like these. Look for levers connecting up and down movements with circular ones in steam engines and pumps.
- Our bones are levers which turn the small contractions of our muscles into larger movements in many directions.

pp 22–23 Paper plate gears
- Explain that gears, like levers, are used to make forces or movements bigger or to change their directions. The little wheel turns much faster than the big one (and in the other direction) but needs less force to move it.
- Look at a bicycle together. The chain connects two toothed wheels, like gears. The big force you use to make your pedals go round once, turns your back wheel round several times.

pp 24–25 Rocket launch
- An elastic material is one which goes back to its original shape after it has been stretched or squeezed. Explain that when you stretch the elastic band with the tube, you give it stored energy. When you let the tube go, the stored energy is released and fires the rocket.

Index

Thank you!

The author would like to thank junior technologists Andrew, Charlie, Ellen Rose, Emily, Francesca, Kate, Laura and Samuel for their work on the projects; and Christopher, Gareth, Jamie, Nana, Rachel, Ella, Bronwyn, Hannah, Dean and Daniel for appearing in the photographs. Many thanks too to the teaching staff at St Luke's Terrace CE Infants School, Downs Infant School, St Bartholomew's CE First School, Davigdor Infants School, St John the Baptist RC First School and Stanford Infants School for their patience and co-operation. Thanks are also due to Halfords of Western Road, Brighton, for lending the children's bike which appears on p. 12.

The author is grateful to Hugh and to her own children, Thomas, Kate and Harry, for all their help and encouragement.

Picture credits

The projects were all photographed specially by Zul Mukhida. Other pictures were supplied by: RNLI, p. 6 (Dave Trotter); ZEFA, p. 14 (Hubrich), p. 18 (W.H. Mueller); Zul Colour Library, pp. 4, 16, 22.